The Tree of Healing
of Lost Love
and Missed Opportunity

Steven Fleming

ISBN: 13:978-1974038756

Published By: Katye Anna SoulWorks Spring Grove PA 17362

The Tree of

Healing

of LOST LOVE
& MISSED OPPORTUNITY

Told by Steven R. Fleming

Reviews
The Healing Tree of Lost Love
and Missed Opportunity

"Wonderful! A rich, relevant, and well-written tale that has applications for anyone who is human, who has loved, and who has lost someone or something precious to them. In other words, it applies to all of us!

Congratulations and best wishes for getting the word of this amazing story out to the wide audience that it so deserves." *Vicki Duncan*

****

"For some who experience cataclysmic trauma, renewed spiritual perspective and energy cannot be given directly— only indirectly, through parable and metaphor. In this real but fictional story, Steven Fleming draws you into seeing lost love and missed opportunities as doorways to new life. This radical newness may creep up on you bit by bit. Only in the tincture of time you may realize that your life is re-deemed, re-valued." -- Kent Ira Groff, writer, poet, retreat leader, and spiritual guide living in Colorado. His book Honest to God *Prayer: Spirituality as Awareness, Empowerment, Relinquishment and Paradox* and others are available online at www.LinkYourSpirituality.com

"Wow. Wow, wow, wow, wow, and wow! I am astounded, speechless, and very moved by your story. Wow, again. There is no doubt in my mind that this is divinely inspired. Victoria D. (Pastoral Counselor and Author, Maryland)

****

"What an inspired story and has multiple possibilities for therapeutic and personal healing. As a therapist, the Seven Gates provide an excellent framework for those clients which have experienced tremendous losses and are searching for hope and healing in the future. Well done and thank you!" *Dee Hirsh*

****

"Thank you for having the creativity, the fortitude and the will to craft your wonderful story of healing. It describes, in a gorgeous metaphor, one of the most humbling and beneficial experiences that we humans take in life, sometimes over and over...the journey from pain to healing to possibility that I have seen so many clients travel. Nice work!" Marie Erb-Crow

****

"As a teacher of soul and an author, I am always looking for resources for my students and clients. I started recommending "The Tree of Healing of Lost Love and Missed Opportunity" for my clients who are moving through grief as well as other losses in their lives. The author's insight and words of wisdom will help many to begin to let go of the past, and begin to see a future life of joy." Katye Anna

ACKNOWLEDGEMENTS:

I wish to acknowledge and thank the following:

Brenda Kay Fleming, who helped me with many details, suggestions, and proof-reading throughout the long and challenging process of completing this story for actual publication

Dian Nelson, who professionally reviewed and edited the original manuscript and made many helpful comments and corrections

Rhonda Dyson, a talented friend, who worked with me to produce the wonderful graphics that illustrate the story. You can find Rhonda on Facebook at Rhonda-Dyson-Photography.

Vicky Hollar Duncan, Ginger O'Connell, Sanford Alwine, Lois Richwine, Kent Groff, and Vicky Cairns who read the various drafts. Each encouraged me with suggestions and affirmations to get this into print because each felt it could help others in their life journeys.

And my mother, Marie Kitzmiller Fleming Barnhart, who has encouraged me throughout my life to keep moving forward, facing life's challenges and disappointments with courage and hope.

■ _Steven Fleming_

"...I am come that they might have life, and that they might have it more abundantly." --- *John 10:10b, KJV*

Go here to purchase an E-Book copy:
http://healingtreeoflostlove.com/

  To read the blog, learn about seminars, workshops, and other resources go to:

http://healingtreeoflostlove.com

To contact the author:
mail@SRFLifeRetirementCoach.com

Contents

Pathway
to the *Summit*

Chapter 1
Pathway to The Summit

IN A FAR-AWAY LAND not easily reached is The Tree of Healing for those burdened by thoughts of lost love or missed opportunity. It is reported The Tree is high upon a mountaintop, with endless views in every direction of astonishing clarity and beauty. A long, winding, well-trodden ancient stone path leads from the lush meadows below to a flat, rocky summit where this Tree has stood since before human time began.

As one approaches this place there is an endless line of pilgrims, stretching far into the distant reaches of those meadows, many making their way in solemn, pensive silence toward the beginning of the path to the summit.

They come – women and men, younger and older, from every country and nation. Some are short, some tall, some well-proportioned, some not. Onlookers might describe some of these persons as attractive, while others might be considered plain, perhaps even unattractive. It doesn't matter.

They are all here for the same purpose. Someplace, somehow, someway, for some reason, they are dealing with a lost opportunity or a lost love.

If asked, more than a few pilgrims would say they have had multiple such hard experiences, as if life has piled them on one after another until they feel virtually crushed to the ground.

Others have had but one. Their wounds, however, are just as deep and the pain just as excruciating. All harbor some sense their future is somehow bleak, the days ahead dark and empty.

For a number of these pilgrims, their lost love or missed opportunity is fresh in time and memory.

They can barely think of anything else: hour after hour, day after day. Consumed. Obsessed.

Others have carried around their feelings, struggles, pain and disappointments for many years, perhaps most of a lifetime. Yet, even so many years after the event, a song, a sound, a place, a smell, a photograph, an unexpected memory dredges their pain back up from where they had tried to bury it long ago. Or rebury it last month. Or even yesterday.

Regardless of how deep they try to make the burial hole, however, those experiences and related pain resurface again and again in cruel, sad, dispiriting repetition.

But they have come, these pilgrims, on a journey to find out if the stories they had heard about The Tree of Healing of Lost Love or Missed Opportunity were true.

In this place, someone had told them, people just like them had found peace, solace, and healing.

Some of the many pilgrims had just about given up hope for true healing of mind, spirit, and heart. They came, hoping – perhaps praying -- there was something to the story that would make the long and arduous journey worthwhile.

When a pilgrim reaches the beginning of that ancient pathway winding upwards, there is a large moss-covered stone marker with letters hand-carved deeply into the rock. What is amazing is the fact that, regardless of one's language or even ability to read, everyone who looks at the weathered lettering understands the words carved thereupon:

"May You Find the Peace You Seek"

At the start of the pathway, there is also a clear, safe spring-fed stone fountain hung with worn, bronze cups to quench thirst. Nearby sit baskets of freshly baked bread, the loaves still warm, and wonderful varieties of cheeses for nourishment. Not everyone notices, however, that the fountain and baskets of bread and cheeses are always full and pure, even though countless pilgrims have already passed that way and partaken that same day.

Seated on a stone bench just past the water and food at what is the true beginning of the ancient stone pathway, is a Guide. As each pilgrim approaches, he or she is greeted with these words:

"Welcome to the ancient path leading up to The Tree of Healing of Lost Love and Missed Opportunity. You have wisely chosen to make this journey. At the summit, you will experience healing in the way that you are seeking and in the way that you need."

"For many of you, this is your first such pilgrimage. For others, this is a second, third or more time you have come to seek solace, peace, and healing due to painful experiences at various times in their lives.

Regardless, each time, the experience will be different in some way. All are welcome to make this pilgrimage as often as needed."

"Beyond this point, time has no meaning. Take what is necessary for your journey. **Do not be anxious** about what you shall eat or what you shall drink. Safe water and nourishment, places to rest, and anything else you require, will be provided as you need them. Focus on your journey. The journey will not be easy, but the reward for completion will be great."

"To reach the summit and complete the journey, you must pass successfully through each of the Seven Gates. Each Gate leads to a different experience important to your individual successful healing. You will find a Guide at each Gate who will tell you everything you need to know for the next part of your journey."

"I should caution you, however. Many find they do not progress smoothly and directly to the summit. Perhaps they need more time to pass a Gate. Some will discover they have to go back down the pathway and re-start their journey at an earlier place in order to go higher. And, sadly, some will never complete the journey because passing through one of the Seven Gates is too hard or requires more from them than they expected, and they give up."

The Guide concludes with these words: "May You Find the Peace You Seek."

At this beginning point, one can gaze upward at the pathway filled with a seemingly endless number of pilgrims. No one can see the ending point at the high summit. If one watches carefully, the pilgrims ahead disappear from view from time to time as they traverse the well-worn stones that pave the way.

One would think that such a line of people of varying ages and sizes and abilities would move at a snail's pace, or worse, but that would be wrong.

As each pilgrim begins his or her journey past the welcoming stone marker and first Guide, the pace of travel feels just right. No one trips over another, nor does one overtake another. The line just flows as if guided by some unseen "journey-to-the-summit" controller who speeds up or slows down each person to avoid collisions, thereby neither straining nor stressing them unnecessarily.

FIRST GATE

The
Pool of *Memories*

Chapter 2
First Gate
The Pool of Memories

NOT FAR FROM the entrance, but beyond initial sight, is the First Gate. And there is a stone marker with deeply carved letters, quite similar to the sign at the start of the stone path. When pilgrims are close enough to the First Gate, they can see what the sign says:

"First Gate: The Pool of Memories"

A Guide greets each pilgrim with these words:

"Welcome, pilgrim. Further down, you will find a pool of water. Once there, you will know what to do." "After you finish, and take all of the time you need, you will be shown what direction to take next." "May You Find the Peace You Seek"

Pilgrims pass through The Gate of Memories and head along the path. As they progress, there is an ever-louder, strange cacophony of familiar sounds ahead. Rounding a bend in the path, they first see the far edges of a huge, beautiful pool of crystal-clear water.

As they get closer, they see the front edge of the pool is lined with fellow pilgrims, all looking intently into the water.

A moss-covered sign is next to the water. It says simply:

"The Pool of Memories"

There is always space for each new pilgrim at the water's edge. As each takes her or his place and looks into the troubled waters, one of two things happens.

Either the waters become still and they see in the now mirror-like water's surface images of past painful events, persons, places, or some combination of these.

Or, as the waters continue to be troubled, they see little or nothing at all regardless of how intently or how long they look. For those who do see more than a fleeting glance, memories and their details often are revealed as they gaze deeper and longer into the pool. These memories of images, persons, and places unfold in no certain order and at varying speeds. A few, especially painful memories replay over and over and over with ever more disturbing effect.

Some memories are seen in vivid colors. Others appear in neutral or gray tones. Some are in black and white. Some have accompanying sounds, smells, or even physical sensations of touch.

For those able to see something of significance, this is an important step of their journey to The Tree of Healing of Lost Love and Missed Opportunity.

For those who see nothing or get only a brief, fleeting glimpse, this becomes a bitter, frustrating experience. They look around to see what others are doing. But one can only see one's own memories, if any, and not what others may – or may not – see.

Those who see nothing, or very little, at some point simply give up. They will follow others leaving the Pool of Memories.

In both instances, however, the sound heard approaching the pool of crystal-clear water is now understood: It is the sound of human crying.

The strange cacophony of sounds is that of innumerable broken-hearted souls joined together in a sad chorus of personal pain, anguish, and regret.

Moreover, each pilgrim now sees the source of the crystal-clear waters of the Pool of Memories.

The pool is filled – and constantly refilled – with an unending flow of human tears. Teardrop by teardrop, painful memory by painful memory, the Pool is replenished for pilgrims yet to reach this place.

One can see the tears on many of their cheeks. Sobs issue from many mouths. At some point, each pilgrim decides to move on following in the direction of others leaving the Pool of Memories behind.

As the sound of human grief and anguish slowly fades in the distance, around a bend, the pathway splits. A stone sign points in one of two directions, depending on what happened to each pilgrim at the Pool of Memory.

The sign reads:

THIS WAY UP to The Tree of Healing of Lost Love or Missed Opportunity. Those pilgrims who were able to see and re-live significant moments at the Pool of Memories continue to move up the ancient pathway to the next

Gate. If they have not been able to see much, if anything, the sign reads: THIS WAY.

Perhaps they were unwilling to spend the time at the Pool needed to truly see and experience their painful memories. Or they were afraid to face the pain those memories would bring.   As they go around the bend, they find themselves back at the bottom of the mountain. There, they will have to decide whether to try again, or quit.

SECOND GATE

Place of *Anger*

Chapter 3
Second Gate
Place of Anger

CONTINUING UP THE pathway toward the summit, the pilgrims directed that way as the path splits come, after a short journey, upon the next of the Seven Gates.

An ancient stone marker with deeply carved letters reads:

"Second Gate: The Place of Anger"

Entering through this Second Gate, a Guide awaits with simple instructions.

"Welcome, pilgrim. Farther down, you will find a pile of stones. Once there, you will know what to do."

"After you finish – and take all of the time you need -- you will be shown what direction to take next."

"May You Find the Peace You Seek"

As pilgrims continue on, they hear the sounds of rocks thudding and things breaking and people straining, huffing and puffing.

Rounding the corner, there is a moss-covered sign which reads: "The Place of Anger."

Beyond, there are countless pilgrims with piles of rocks at their feet. They are taking one rock after another and throwing them at something no one else can see.

Getting closer, one still cannot see what their targets are, but the loud thuds and sounds of things breaking are audible to all.

Watching a bit longer, pilgrims observe that some throw just a few rocks and then move along, while others keep picking up one rock after another and hurling it into space.

Yet, the pilgrims note, as they keep throwing they appear more weary, frustrated, and exhausted even as they struggle to pick up yet another rock and heave it.

A pile of rocks appears at the pilgrims' feet, and they wonder where to throw them.

Looking up from the rock pile, they are startled by images within range with bulls-eyes on them.   Some are the same images pilgrims saw in the Pool of Memories.

For many, these memories incite within each person some level of frustration, anger, rage, and even the desire for revenge.

It could be the face of a parent who always belittled them or blocked them from following their dreams. It could be the face of a co-worker or boss whose actions cost them the opportunity of a lifetime.

Perhaps it is someone who cheated them out of money for their children's education or their retirement. The image may well be a lover, husband, or wife who mistreated them or broke their heart by their actions, words, or, perhaps, a deep betrayal.

In fact, it could even be their own face, recalling something that they did that messed up their opportunity or love relationship.

For some, the target appears as a short, endless-loop movie documenting a sequence of events in which – if they had just made one different choice – they believe their life would have been richer, fuller, deeper, more satisfying.

They didn't make that choice, and the opportunities never came again. But the memory of that lost love or opportunity and the resulting pain, the deep hurt, keeps playing back over and over and over again.

Regardless of the target, most pilgrims pick up at least a few rocks and throw them at the target. Some rocks miss, but most make contact.

For a few pilgrims, that's enough. They have gotten that "out of their system," so to speak.

They move on along the pathway. They have done what they needed to do.

But others can't stop.

Again and again they hurl the rocks, as if driven to knock the person or memory down forever, destroying the person, the memory, thinking that will somehow ease the pain and erase the memories.

But an interesting thing begins to happen. While all of the rocks are about the same size, the more of them thrown, the heavier the next one becomes. It comes to the point that one cannot lift a rock with one hand – now it takes two.

And those heavier and heavier rocks don't travel as far, so fewer and fewer hit the target. Then, the rocks become so heavy that pilgrims often drop them on their toes or strain their back or collapse from exhaustion.

Finally, regardless of how angry they feel, they cannot even pick up any rock, no matter how hard they try. They step back from the rock pile and catch their breath. Some will resume trying to throw rocks, repeating the fruitless effort.

For most pilgrims who reach this point, however, the truth finally dawns upon them: Thoughts, feelings, and actions of anger and revenge really, truly only punish one person: themselves.

Continuing to hold onto their anger and desire for revenge is not the way to find the peace that they seek.

Over time, when each decides, the pilgrims move on, following in the direction of others who have left their rock piles behind.

As the sounds of rocks thudding and things breaking fades away, around a bend, the pathway splits.

A stone sign points in one of two directions, depending on whether the pilgrim has been able to let go of anger and the need for revenge.

If they have, the sign reads:

THIS WAY UP to The Tree of Healing. Those pilgrims continue to move up the ancient pathway to the next Gate.

If they have not, the sign reads: THIS WAY. As they go around a bend, they find themselves somewhere back down the mountain.

Perhaps they need to re-visit the Pool of Memories, for something about the prior visit there was left unfinished. Or they find themselves at the bottom, as if just starting their journey.

There, they will have to decide whether to try again, or quit.

One hopes, however, that if they can't get past a Gate, when they go back down the mountain they will, at some point, begin their journey to The Tree of Lost Love or Missed Opportunity again.

THIRD GATE

Waterfall
of *Understanding*

Chapter 4
Third Gate
Waterfall of Understanding

AS THE PILGRIMS continue their journey toward the Summit, after a reasonable distance of travel for each person, they come upon another of the Seven Gates.

An ancient sign with deeply carved letters says simply:

"Third Gate: The Waterfall of Understanding"

Entering through this Third Gate, a Guide awaits with instructions.

"Welcome, pilgrim. Further down, you will find a waterfall. Once there, you will know what to do."

"After you finish, and take all of the time you need, you will be shown what direction to take next."

"May You Find the Peace You Seek."

As pilgrims continue on the ancient, well-worn path, they hear the growing sounds of rushing water splashing over rocks. Rounding the corner, where the sound of the waterfall is now quite loud, there is an ancient stone sign.

It reads: "The Waterfall of Understanding"

Ahead, pilgrims are gathered. Each is looking intently toward the sound of the waterfall, but a heavy mist obscures the view of the actual waterfall as the pilgrims approach and they take their place among the other pilgrims.

There is always room for the next pilgrim to stand and look into the mist that is obscuring the waterfall. Most peer expectantly and intently toward the soothing, yet insistent sounds.

For many pilgrims, as they continue to peer into the heavy mist, an image or images begin to appear formed out of the droplets of the mist itself.

Each pilgrim can see only her or his images and no one else's. Most of these images relate to what they saw in the Pool of Memories or at the Place of Anger earlier in their journey.

However, this time, as the images appear, there is a wider, larger view provided to each pilgrim. The images now are viewed in a larger context, or so it seems.

As the images enlarge, they provide a birds-eye view of the events, places and people surrounding the experiences that caused their pain and feelings of loss.

Now, at the Waterfall of Understanding, pilgrims begin to sense the fullness of what was really happening at that time, place, or with that person or persons. They see clearly, often for the first time, that there were many other factors at work behind the scenes that contributed to their lost love or missed opportunity.

For example, some now understand that a parent or parents did their best to provide for, care for and love them.

They also now understand those parents had their own pain and inadequacies which led them to act in ways that were hurtful, sometimes even abusive.

Or a boss's action is now seen in a wider perspective. What happened that day was nothing more than a business decision made at some unknown higher level. Their boss was left with the disagreeable task of firing someone considered a friend or well-respected co-worker. They truly agonized about the well-being of those being terminated.

Or a lover, husband, wife, or close friend who left them behind or betrayed their trust in some way or was unable to meet the pilgrim's deeper needs over time, was actually enmeshed in pain and struggle at the time.

These pilgrims come to understand those persons could not adequately handle the pressure of the relationship in some way or other.

As a pilgrim comes to understand the many dimensions of reality surrounding particular hurtful, painful experiences, each begins to see and comprehend the past in new, more hopeful and healing ways. Hearts and emotions soften. The pilgrim begins to find some peace related to lost love or missed opportunity.

At that very moment of true understanding, the heavy mists part. The sight of the stunningly beautiful waterfall overwhelms with a sense of relief and peace.

In the spectacle of the ever-flowing water and soothing sounds, one comes to see his or her own life history and experiences in a new light.

If asked how they feel at that moment of revelation, many would say that for the first time they truly understand their lost love or missed opportunity. Before, they could only look at their past through what seemed like a heavy mist of confusion, questions, and pain.

Now, a much-needed sense of goodwill has come upon them. Some need only a little peering into the mist for this gift of understanding to come. Others need much more time.

For some, however, the heavy mists never part. The spectacular waterfall is never seen. These pilgrims have also looked intently into the fog-like clouds of mist, hearing the sounds beyond. Although they see images in the mist, they are unable, for some reason to view those images in the larger context.

Some are too focused on their own pain and hurt, unable to step back and allow the meaning of what has happened to be revealed.

Some, frankly, don't want to see or understand. For some reason, these pilgrims are not ready to delve more deeply into the circumstances and dynamics of their painful life experiences and relationships in order to pass this Gate.

To seek true understanding of one's lost love or missed opportunity is to realize that, in the end, most people do their best with what they have at the time. That means, of course, more than a few times the inevitable human inadequacies all carry create pain and loss for someone else.

When ready, each pilgrim moves away from The Waterfall of Understanding and follows the other pilgrims who are also leaving. As the sound of the waterfall fades away, around another bend, the pathway splits.

A moss-covered stone sign points in one of two directions, depending on whether the pilgrim has reached a place of understanding, or not.

For those who have, the sign reads:

THIS WAY UP to The Tree of Healing of Lost Love or Missed Opportunity. Those pilgrims continue to move up the ancient pathway to the next Gate.

If they have not, the sign reads: THIS WAY. As they go around a bend, they find themselves somewhere back down the mountain.

Perhaps they need to re-visit the Gate of Anger and work through more of those feelings. Perhaps they need to return to the Pool of Memories.

They may find themselves at the bottom, as if just starting their journey.

When unable to pass one Gate, something about a prior stop along the way has been left unfinished.

There, they will have to decide whether to try again or quit.

FOURTH GATE

The Maze of Acceptance

Chapter 5
Fourth Gate
The Maze of Acceptance

AS THE PILGRIMS continue their journey toward the summit, at a reasonable walk for each person, they come upon another of the Seven Gates.

A moss-covered sign with deeply carved letters reads simply:

"Fourth Gate: The Maze of Acceptance"

Entering through this Gate, a Guide awaits with simple instructions.

"Welcome, pilgrim. Further down, you will find an ancient maze with one entrance in and one entrance out. Once there, you will know what to do."

"After you finish, and take all of the time you need, you will be shown what direction to take next."

"May You Find the Peace You Seek"

Pilgrims pass the Guide and follow the well-worn, ancient stone path. As they get closer to the maze, they hear faint, then louder sounds of voices repeating words in countless languages.

At the entrance to the maze is a stone sign which reads: "The Maze of Acceptance."

Since there is only one way in, the pilgrims follow those before them into the maze, wondering what experience is ahead. As is always true on the ancient stone path itself, everyone moves at the appropriate pace without interfering with other pilgrims in their walk.

The maze must be thousands of years old. The walls of the passageways are many feet thick and made of a dense evergreen plant. They rise up what seems to be twenty or more feet toward the sky.

As the pilgrims progress into the maze, they come to the first decision point. Go left? Or right? At that moment, an image or images from the past appears to each pilgrim.

Just like the images at the Pool of Memory, the Place of Anger or the Waterfall of Understanding, no one can see anyone else's images. Some see just a single, static image. Others may see something like a photograph album of a particular time, event, person, or place being opened page by page.

Still others see what are best described as short movies or video clips recounting some lost love or missed opportunity.

This time, however, the experience of the images is full and in great detail. Smell. Sound. Touch. All of the senses that apply to the particular image or images are fully experienced. In addition, for those who have progressed this far, the ability to more fully understand their experiences gained at the Waterfall of Understanding is quite real and comforting. They begin to confront their lost love or missed opportunity in fullness and depth most had never felt before.

If a pilgrim, at that moment of decision, is able to acknowledge within his or her heart truthfully and honestly "Now I accept the reality of my lost love or missed opportunity," the images move in the direction leading out of the maze.

Then they disappear.

If, however, at that moment the pilgrim cannot say "Now I accept the reality of my lost love or missed opportunity" truthfully and honestly, the images lead in the opposite direction towards a dead end and then disappear.

As the pilgrims move through The Maze of Acceptance, they will come to many points of decision and must choose whether to go left or right. Each time, the same images appear. Each time, the pilgrim has to affirm acceptance of their realities by saying, "Now I accept the reality of my lost love or missed opportunity."

If the pilgrim can say that with integrity, the images move again in the direction leading out before disappearing.

Pilgrims who wind up at a dead end realize they must return to the prior decision point and go the other way. From there they, like the others, move on to the next decision point where they again have to choose either right or left. Their images reappear as before.

At this point, they have another chance to say, "Now I accept the reality of my lost love or missed opportunity." If they can say those words honestly and forthrightly, the images move in the direction out and then disappear.

If they cannot, the images move in the other direction toward another dead end.

This cycle of decision points continues time after time for each pilgrim. Each decision point leads closer to the only exit. For many, the same images appear throughout the maze. For some, several different images appear before exiting the maze. The most important one for their journey is what shows first and continues to show until the pilgrim's acceptance is honest and truthful, deep and real. Then, the second most important one for the journey appears, and the pilgrim has to make a similar decision.

And so it continues as the pilgrim progresses through The Maze of Acceptance.

As one gets deeper into the maze, it becomes clear what the once-faint sounds of voices repeating words in countless languages their heard were as they approached. It was the words, softly or loudly spoken at each decision point that make up what one might call a chant:

"Now I accept the reality of my lost love or missed opportunity."

Finally, regardless of whether one has been truly able to say those words, each pilgrim comes to the only exit of The Maze of Acceptance. As each pilgrim follows the others out, and the sounds of voices fade away, around another bend the pathway splits.

A moss-covered stone sign points in one of two directions, depending on whether the pilgrim has reached a true, inner acceptance of the lost love or missed opportunity.

For those who have, the sign reads:

THIS WAY UP to the Tree of Healing. Those pilgrims continue to move up the ancient pathway to the next Gate.

If they have not, the sign reads: THIS WAY.

As they go around a bend, they find themselves somewhere back down the mountain. Perhaps they need to re-visit the Waterfall of Understanding or the Place of Anger to work through more of those feelings. Perhaps they need to return to the Pool of Memories.

When unable to complete one Gate, something along the way has been left unfinished.

Or, they may find themselves at the bottom, as if just starting their journey.

There, they will have to decide whether to try again or quit.

FIFTH GATE

Garden
of *Forgiveness*

Chapter 6
Fifth Gate
Garden of Forgiveness

AS THE PILGRIMS continue their journey toward the summit, at a reasonable distance for each person, they come upon the fifth of the Seven Gates.

An ancient sign with deeply carved letters says simply:

"Fifth Gate: The Garden of Forgiveness"

As each pilgrim enters this fifth Gate, a Guide awaits with simple instructions.

"Welcome, pilgrim. Further down, you will find a garden to walk through, for you to meditate in, for you to enjoy. Once there, you will know what to do."

"After you finish, and take all of the time you need, you will be shown what direction to take next."

"May You Find the Peace You Seek."

The pilgrims pass by the Guide and follow the ancient stone pathway as directed. Around a bend in the path, they come upon what appears as a barren plot of parched ground. It is overgrown with weeds and thorns, strewn with pieces of broken pottery and rocks. Hardly the garden they expected!

Adjacent to the dismal plot of ground is a weathered sign reading: "The Garden of Forgiveness."

The stone pathway leads through this bleak spot and beyond. Most pilgrims are bewildered. Surely this cannot be the right place?

Many stop and stare at the parched ground strewn with rocks and shattered pottery, overgrown with weeds and thorns. A few hurry along, thinking that somewhere ahead must be the real destination. They may never know what they missed.

For those who do stop and look around, however, a few notice the rocks seem familiar somehow. How is that possible? Most have never been to this place before, yet those stones seem so familiar. Then it dawns on them: they look like the same rocks they had thrown at the Place of Anger. And the broken pieces of pottery and other objects? Could they be the remnants of what was heard breaking as those rocks were thrown? Are these remnants of dishes and pots and vases actually symbolic of home, career, or relationships smashed to pieces in rage, anger, revenge?

Then, as happened many times before, an image or images appear to each pilgrim who took the time to stop, meditate, and ponder this strange Garden of Forgiveness. This time the images do not stir up the same reactions and emotions as before.

For having been to the Waterfall of Understanding and through the Maze of Acceptance, these images now bring a great opportunity. Pilgrims realize that the next step in their journey to The Tree of Healing is actually the answer to a simple, yet powerful, question they hear deep within:

"Can you forgive others – and just as importantly, forgive yourself – for whatever was the cause of your lost love or missed opportunity?"

The impact of that question along with the image or images now given to those who have both come to understand and accept the reality of their lost love or missed opportunity, is often overwhelming. The reactions of those who now understand the deep need to give and seek forgiveness deep within their hearts, minds, and souls are powerful.

Many pilgrims fall to their knees as they cry out, "I forgive!" or "Please forgive me!" Uncounted numbers shed bittersweet tears that combine the feelings of great release and relief with a draining away of the last vestiges of bitterness or self-accusation that has imprisoned them for so long.

As the tears of those now-humble pilgrims hit the barren ground, something mystical begins to happen. Where a tear has fallen, a tiny plant shoot appears and grows rapidly into a beautiful, radiant, fragrant blossom. One plant. Ten plants. A thousand plants. Ten thousand plants! One hundred thousand plants!! There are too many to count!!!

Some pilgrims go out into the barren plot to pick up rocks and pieces of broken pottery, almost as if performing an act of penance. As they move through the grounds weeping with joy and relief, their tears raise up even more new plants.

Soon the Garden of Forgiveness is no longer a barren wasteland, but instead a lush riot of colors and fragrances that overwhelms the senses and sets one's heart free. If you look in the distance, at the back of The Garden of Forgiveness, there is now a beautiful stone fence into which pieces of broken pottery have been deftly placed in stunning patterns.

A gentle, soothing breeze comes through the now beautiful Garden of Forgiveness. Many pilgrims laugh and dance and sing! They feel like captives who have just been released!

At some point, after they have laughed and danced and sung as much as they needed or wanted, the pilgrims move on through and out of the Garden of Forgiveness on the well-worn stone pathway.   Those pilgrims who come behind them find – a barren plot of ground. Until....until the cycle starts over again.

How could it get better than this, many pilgrims think, as they continue on. Yet, they know there are seven Gates. The Garden of Forgiveness is just the fifth.

Around another bend, the pathway splits.

An ancient stone sign points in one of two directions, depending on whether the pilgrim has been able to truly forgive others or themselves as evidenced by his or her experience in the Garden of Forgiveness.

For those who have, the sign reads: THIS WAY UP to The Tree of Healing. Those pilgrims continue to move up the ancient pathway to the next Gate.

If they have not, the sign reads: THIS WAY. As they go around a bend, they find themselves somewhere back down the mountain. Perhaps they need to re-visit the Maze of Acceptance, the Waterfall of Understanding, or the Place of Anger to work through more of their feelings? Perhaps they need to return to the Pool of Memories.

When unable to complete one Gate, something has been left unfinished.

Or, they may find themselves at the bottom, as if just starting their journey.

There, they will have to decide whether to try again or quit.

SIXTH GATE

Grand Courtyard
of the
Tree of *Healing*

Chapter 7
Sixth Gate
Grand Courtyard of The
Tree of Healing

AS THE PILGRIMS continue their journey toward the summit, at a reasonable distance for each person, they come upon the next of the Seven Gates.

A sign with deeply carved letters reads:

"Sixth Gate: The Grand Courtyard of the Tree of Healing"

As a pilgrim enters through this sixth Gate, a Guide awaits with simple instructions.

"Welcome, pilgrim. You are at the summit of the holy mountain and possibly close to the end of your journey. There is just one more Gate after this one to successfully complete your pilgrimage."

"Just ahead you will find the Grand Courtyard of The Tree of Healing of Lost Love and Missed Opportunity. Once in the Courtyard, you will know what to do."

"After you finish, and take all of the time you need, you will be shown what direction to take next."

"May You Find the Peace You Seek."

As pilgrims follow the stone pathway, they come to an entry way in a towering wall. Up to this point, due to the angle of the pathway and the height of the towering wall, they cannot see anything inside the walls, only the sky.

Carved over this entrance are the words: "Grand Courtyard of The Tree of Healing."

As pilgrims enter through the sixth Gate, they are confronted by the amazing sight of an enormous tree soaring into the sky and spreading its innumerable, huge branches. It is the focal point of the circular Grand Courtyard, with its many seats on the inside of the stone wall, all facing the Tree. Many pilgrims are already in their seats, gazing forward in a variety of moods and reactions.

As has been true throughout the journey, there is always a place for the next pilgrim.

Each one is soon seated facing the Tree.

Within the Grand Courtyard there is no sound.

No breeze. No birds. No animals.

The temperature is just right for each pilgrim, seats so comfortable as if carved to each particular body shape and size.   Nothing in this place is allowed to disturb the pilgrim's attention, thoughts, feelings, senses, and reactions.

There is a deep silence as each of the pilgrims contemplates and reflects, in his or her own way and time, The Tree of Healing of Lost Love and Missed Opportunity.

The only possible distraction is a subtle sense of other pilgrims, at their own paces, getting up and moving toward either the ancient Grand Courtyard wall or The Tree - or both - then disappearing from view through another Gate opposite the one through which they entered.

The TREE of *Healing*

Chapter 8

The Tree of Healing

EVERY PILGRIM HAS the same view of The Tree when first arriving.

It is barren, naked, exposed -- as if in the deep of a winter season's sleep.

Upon closer examination of the Tree in this winter season perspective, detail after detail is more fully revealed. Beside the almost unimaginable size of The Tree in terms of height and breadth, it shoots upward from a massive gnarled root system that goes down into the rocky summit hundreds, if not thousands, of feet. No one now viewing the Tree doubts it dates back before human time.

Indeed, one legend circulating among pilgrims is The Tree is an offshoot of the tree of the Knowledge of Good and

Evil that grew in the Garden of Eden. Certainly, as one gazes upon this massive specimen, the idea does not seem out of the realm of possibility.

Looking up through the canopy of branches, one's attention is soon drawn to a large broken limb. That wounded limb is now healed over with the passage of unknown years.

One might speculate what happened to the part of The Tree that broke off? More than a few pilgrims recall stories repeated from one pilgrim to another as they crossed the lush meadows toward the beginning of their ascent.

From a limb of The Tree of Healing, some said, the keel of Noah's ark was made. Others reported its wood was used to make the Ark of the Covenant. Others said that from the shattered branch three crosses were made. No one really knows. Any - or all - are possible.

More details come to the pilgrims as they sit and meditate upon The Tree. The trunk and lower branches, as well as many of the gnarled roots, appear to have carvings on them. Many carvings are in unknown languages or use ancient symbols which are unintelligible in the modern world. One cannot count the heart-shaped carvings with initials inside. Nor can one count the names, dates, places, or other symbols of remembrance carved so deeply into the bark. What is not evident at this moment is how those carvings got there? Or is it possible for others to do the same as part of their own pilgrimage?

It is whispered as pilgrims make their way to the summit that there are only two times of the day when pilgrims can fully understand the meaning of the carvings: at dawn and sunset. In those two moments: one representing promise, the other representing closure, The Tree speaks for and witnesses to the multitude of those who reached this place before. The carvings tell the stories of many of those who completed their arduous journey to The Tree of Healing of Lost Love and Missed Opportunity.

These carvings bear witness to the pilgrims who received the promised great reward. They found the healing they needed in the way they needed it. Now it was each new pilgrim's opportunity to find that same healing. But looking upon the barren, scarred, ageless and enormous tree, first impressions bring little initial comfort.

It is at this moment of uncertainty that words carved deeply into the Grand Courtyard floor, encircling The Tree completely, are revealed. Whatever their language or ability to read, all can understand the timeless message:

"To everything there is a Season, and a time to every purpose under Heaven."

As the pilgrims continue to gaze upon The Tree, still questioning how what they saw before them could really be the Tree of Healing, a subtle change in the Tree's appearance begins. New green shoots with buds of leaves and delicate flowers begin to appear on the canopy of The Tree. Incredibly, the once barren Winter Season Tree is transformed into the Promise of Spring Tree before their amazed eyes. The new growth is a vivid mixture of greens. A slight, steady breeze rises and teases the new growth. The brilliant green leaves shimmer like a billion emeralds as they move. And the fragrance of the pure white blossoms wafts across the Courtyard. The scent, some say, is similar to the tree-harvested resins frankincense and myrrh.

Spring season birds begin to appear around, and in, The Tree, building large numbers of nests. Their comings and goings, their bewitching, unique birdsongs, and their nests filled with young fledglings unceasingly chirping to be fed, all mix into a spring-time symphony celebrating the new life now resident in The Tree.

Listen! Did you hear that? Many pilgrims think they hear something in the gentle breezes. Yes, there is a message carried by the breezes. Do you hear it?

"Come, all ye that are heavy laden…."

For many of the pilgrims, this sight and experience breathe a renewed vitality deep into their being. It is as if they, too, were being reborn as The Tree transforms from its deep winter sleep to new life and hope symbolized by spring leaves and blossoms. Empty, barren places in heart and soul are slowly filling with promises of a new vitality eerily similar to their experiences in the Garden of Forgiveness, only deeper and more permanent.

And then, as the pilgrim continued to meditate upon The Tree and ponder its surprising transformation, a second change begins. The Promise of Spring Tree is slowly transformed into the Fullness of Summer Tree. The Tree, once barren, then filled with new spring growth, now bursts into full summer leaf. Large leaves. Enormous leaves in deeper, richer greens cast comforting shade and bring a refreshing coolness upon the bright sunlit Grand Courtyard filled with pilgrims.

The warm energy of the sun is soaked up by The Tree in a timeless process, providing its own nourishment, as well as providing fresh air. Carbon dioxide is photosynthesized molecule after molecule into pure, life-giving oxygen.

What was a gentle spring breeze now becomes a more steady summer wind, stimulating the body, mind, and spirit. Leaves move more actively in this wind, making a soothing rustling sound that seems to wash away human care and anxiety.

Larger birds, including hawks and bald eagles as well as tiny darting hummingbirds, are now seen in, around, and above The Tree. Some great birds gracefully soar toward the heavens, their wings uplifted by seasonal winds, the spirits of pilgrims soaring along with them.

It is also when The Tree is viewed in its season of summer that pilgrims notice for the first time the sound of water flowing. Directing their attention to the sounds, they observe streams of water going under and over and around the gnarled root system.

The source of the water is a grouping of ever-flowing springs swelling up directly under The Tree. The individual streams, some say, run under and converge just outside of the Grand Courtyard. There, they form two branches of the fabled River of Life.

One branch runs down the mountainside the pilgrims climbed up to feed the Waterfall of Understanding before draining into the lush meadows below. The other branch goes down the opposite way, forming another waterfall before disappearing into the earth and becoming an underground river watering distant lands.

It is also in this summer season of The Tree that among the roots and safely above the spring waters are seen enormous chests. Inside the ancient chests, one can distinguish various artifacts left behind by pilgrims over the eons.

There are rings, often engraved with a name or a date.

Bracelets and necklaces and cameos, some with secret compartments where a locket of hair or a faded miniature photograph or hand-drawn portrait could be found.

Postcards and letters with special meaning.

Toys and trinkets.

Souvenirs of special places, times or events.

Gold coins, pieces of silver, and a widow's mite.

Piles upon piles of remembrances of someone, someplace, sometime, something special and valued -- all left symbolically at the foot of The Tree of Healing of Lost Love and Missed Opportunity.

How all of these things got there is a mystery, but the sight of such an overwhelming display of so many remembrances of people, places, times and opportunities helps each pilgrim put memories into a larger context. In seeing Life in this larger view, they come to understand that the experience of lost love and missed opportunity is part of the human condition.

They find a deeper healing and comfort as they truly begin to realize that they, in their own life experiences, are not alone. Many, many others have trod the same path before them. Many, many others will follow after.

Then, as that reality of human life sinks in and the healing continues, The Tree begins yet another transformation. From The Tree of summer in all of its fullness, The Tree's leaves begin to turn color as the transitional season of fall arrives.

Slowly but surely, the green leaves change into a kaleidoscope of colors beyond even the most gifted artist's palette. These autumn leaves rustle and rattle in the brisk winds coming and going in varying degrees of force.

The birds of summer, having filled their bellies with the abundance of summer provisions, begin to migrate as they have done since the fifth day of Creation. Their songs fade in the distance as they begin their own pilgrimage to another place of safety.

As the summer to fall transition continues, the enormous leaves begin to fall like an offering, reminding one of the ancient biblical text:

"...and the leaves of the tree were for the healing of the nations."

First, just a few leaves flutter to the ground. Then hundreds of leaves. Then thousands of leaves. Then a virtual blizzard of leaves, until much of the base of The Tree, and much of the Grand Courtyard, is covered in a wild, multi-colored carpet. Some leaves float away in the waters of the springs, as if little boats of remembrance of The Tree of Healing of Lost Love and Missed Opportunity being carried to the far ends of the earth on the River of Life.

And, if they have not already grasped the larger message of the Grand Courtyard experience, at this point the pilgrims do: Life is a cycle.

Just like The Tree of Healing has to go through a time of barrenness, then promise, then fullness, then loss - which leads back to a time of barrenness - such is also the human experience. Their lost love and missed opportunities are part of the larger cycle of their lives. They are not unique in these experiences. Many others have similar experiences.

What matters, in the end, is how these experiences shape and mold a person. How they learn to recover from deep pain and loss is vital. Are they willing to see the meaning, find understanding, realize acceptance, and experience forgiveness so they can find the healing that they need in the way they need it?

Many pilgrims will then, for the first time, notice that in the cracks of the high stone wall behind them that forms The Grand Courtyard are countless pieces of paper or parchment or fabric. And they will see, also for the first time, how they got there.

As pilgrims get up from their seats, many turn around and tuck something in their own handwriting into an open crack between the stones.

Perhaps a prayer for themselves or others?

Perhaps a note with the name of a long-lost parent, child, husband, wife, mentor, or love?

Perhaps a verse from a holy book or author that has brought comfort along the way of their life's journey?

There is no way to know what, exactly, is written on them. What is clear is that when a pilgrim deposits his or hers in the wall, evident on their face is a true peace, a true understanding, a true acceptance, a true forgiveness. In other words, a peace that passes all understanding.

Two other things are also revealed in The Tree in its fall season: how the chests are filled, and how the carvings get onto the branches, trunk, and gnarled roots of The Tree. Those pilgrims still seated are now given the ability to see the movement of others in a new, much clearer way.

They see that some pilgrims, who may - or may not - have placed something in the Grand Courtyard wall, approach The Tree. Some put something in the large chests. Others carve something in The Tree. Many do both. Some neither.

For those wishing to leave a remembrance of some kind in the large chests, there are clear, level, dry pathways formed in the gnarled root system that allow one to get close to the trunk. Once there, many unveil their special remembrances from a place of safe-keeping. They lovingly unwrap the treasure from a cloth or take it from a protective box. Looking intently at whatever the artifact of remembrance they have brought, one can observe a wide variety of facial expressions as these pilgrims reflect upon their item of remembrance. Some smile, some cry, some speak to their item with words no one else can hear.

Some bring their remembrance close to their cheeks or give it a soft kiss. A few rub it gently, as if feeling for one last time the physical reality of someone or something very dear to their hearts.

Finally, gently, lovingly they place their item or items of remembrance in a nearby chest, adding to the vast number of other items left behind. They step back, take one last look, perhaps bowing their heads as if praying, wave goodbye, or make a sign of some religious blessing. A few stand at attention, giving a military salute as if honoring a fallen warrior. But all, in their own time, finally turn away and take the smooth, level, dry pathways back to the Grand Courtyard to continue their journey.

For those who wish to carve into The Tree, however, a mystery is discovered. Most pull out a knife or other sharp instrument to make their marks. But try as they may, no tool of human making makes even the slightest scratch upon the branches, trunk, or gnarled roots of The Tree. They try -- some again and again -- to mark The Tree. All attempts have the same result – not even a scratch!

At some point, different for each pilgrim who desires to make a mark, an image appears -- an image of the human hand. In slow motion, the hand reaches down. Fingers are dipped into the streams flowing out from under The Tree as the image reveals the solution to the mystery. To carve something into The Tree, to make their marks, pilgrims must use a finger or fingers that have been dipped in the waters from the source of the River of Life.

With that knowledge revealed, their fingers dripping with the cold spring water, many add their marks of remembrance or celebration or love and affection to the others already there. And, regardless of what the language, date, symbol, or names thus carved into The Tree, all can only read and fully understand these carvings at just two times each day: At sunrise, the time of promise of a new day; and at sunset, the time of closure of one day and anticipation of the next.

In some unspoken way, each pilgrim knows what comes next and how to proceed. At this point, having witnessed The Tree cycle from winter to spring to summer to fall, the pilgrims – all at their own pace and in their own time – rise from their seats facing The Tree.

As each vacates a seat, another pilgrim takes their place and The Tree's cycle starts anew. In fact, every pilgrim sees The Tree uniquely, but all begin with seeing the initial barren, winter Tree.

Some pilgrims, in leaving, turn and place something in the open cracks of the Grand Courtyard stone wall. Some do not. Some move to The Tree, and add their item or items of significance to the large chests at the base. Some do not. Some dip their fingers in the cold streams and carve something onto The Tree. Some do not. Some do all. Some do nothing.

Each may choose if, and what, he or she wishes to do while leaving The Grand Courtyard of The Tree of Healing of Lost Love and Missed Opportunity.

For while such actions may provide an additional way of confirming, celebrating or seeking closure on life's lost love or missed opportunity, each pilgrim must do what his or her heart says must be done. Or not done.

Whatever actions they do or do not take, all who have reached the Grand Courtyard and gazed upon the cycle of The Tree of Healing, will have found the healing they needed in the way they needed it.

As they experienced in their own way and in their own time the cycle of the seasons, inside of each pilgrim the healing power of The Tree was moving to restore them, mend them, soothe them, comfort them.

SEVENTH GATE

The Way to New *Possibilities*

Chapter 9
Seventh Gate
The Way to New Possibilities

WHEN COMPLETED WITH whatever actions they wished to take, all pilgrims move toward the Seventh Gate in the Grand Courtyard wall opposite where they entered.

Carved into the stone above this last of the Gates is a sign. It reads:

"Seventh Gate: The Way to New Possibilities"

As each enters through this Seventh Gate, a Guide awaits with simple instructions.

"Welcome, pilgrim. You will soon reach the Way to New Possibilities, entered through this last of the Seven Gates.

Here, at the very summit of this mountain, the stone pathway leads up to a wide and level place at the top of the Wall of Grand Courtyard. Once there, you will know what to do.

"To exit, walk around the wall. Opposite of where you began when ascending the stairway, there will be another pathway down. After you finish at the top, and take all of the time you need, you will be shown what direction to take next.

"May You Find the Peace You Seek."

The pilgrims ascend the pathway and reach the wide walkway on the top of the Grand Courtyard wall that completely surrounds The Tree of Healing. From this vantage point at the top, one can see across what appears to be forever. As hoped, the view from the top is stunning: endless views of astonishing clarity and beauty. It is almost as if one were viewing from a heavenly place where land, sea and sky merge into one.

What also never leaves one's consciousness up here is the presence of The Tree rising far above the pathway on top of the Grand Courtyard's wall. In fact, The Tree prevents one from looking across the top of the Courtyard to views on the other side. Perhaps this placement is a reminder that even at the summit one cannot see all of life's possibilities. Some realities are always hidden from view.

Up here, pilgrims come to recognize it is only when one experiences true healing of heart, mind, and spirit that one can truly appreciate the magnificent views and possibilities all around us once again. Or for the first time.

After pilgrims first adjust to the amazing view, they realize they are looking in the direction from which they ascended the mountain. There, far in the distance in the lush meadows, is the ever-constant line of other pilgrims seeking The Tree of Healing of Lost Love and Missed Opportunity. Once, they too had traversed the meadow, questioning if the journey would be worth the effort. They remembered wondering, as some said who would never make the attempt, if it was a fairy tale?

They had feared that if the legendary journey turned out to be a fruitless expedition that this new disappointment would only add to their pain, anger, and frustration. Now at the summit, the pilgrims are grateful they made the effort. They had pursued the possibility of finding such a healing place and renewing experience. And they found it!

Pilgrims looking in this direction also clearly see the various Gates through which they had already passed.

First Gate: The Pool of Memories

Second Gate: The Place of Anger and Revenge

Third Gate: The Waterfall of Understanding

Fourth Gate: The Maze of Acceptance

Fifth Gate: The Garden of Forgiveness

Sixth Gate: The Grand Courtyard of The Tree of Healing

As they gaze down upon these places, they see and feel how traversing each Gate has been important to the healing of their lost love or missed opportunity. More than a few smile or chuckle as they recall going back down the mountain to some lower level many times in their pilgrimage. They had repeated the experience of one or more of the Seven Gates over and over before able to move forward. If only they had known what they now know. How much easier the journey would have been!

To be honest, no one could really know beforehand how easy or hard the journey would be, nor how it would turn out. Only by attempting the journey does one find that.

If any pilgrim at the summit were asked "Was the journey worth it?" all would say in one way or another, "Yes! I'm so glad that I made this journey." And they would say that with a countenance on their faces revealing that peace that passes all understanding.

As pilgrims move around the top of the wall of the Grand Courtyard of The Tree, they realize there are two places they cannot see. While the wide and safe walkway at the top has just a low retaining wall on the vista side, the wall on the side facing the courtyard is too high to see over and into the actual Courtyard.

This accomplishes two purposes. First, it means that the pilgrims seated in the Grand Courtyard could neither see nor be disturbed by the sounds and movements of those on the top of the courtyard wall.

Second, it also means that one could only look out away from the center of the Grand Courtyard. At this point in the journey it was time to move on to new possibilities with only the comforting image of The Tree of Healing of Lost Love and Missed Opportunity in the background.

The Tree's image would protect, shelter, and encourage pilgrims as they moved on with their journeys.

As pilgrims move around the walkway toward the pathway down, they begin to look, not in the direction from whence they had come, but out into some new and some familiar, but all glorious, landscapes. Some find the enchanting valleys and hills to their liking, and resolve to go in that direction. Others are drawn to the stunning mountains and high places. Still others note fields of grain, orchards or vineyards that will become part of their new life.

Some are excited to see seas, oceans and sandy beaches. The awesome, stark beauty of desert landscapes pull at the hearts of yet others. Perhaps a city, or a town, or a village, or rural place they see in the distance beckons to them? So many new places and new possibilities!

What all the pilgrims have in common as they ponder the endless views of spectacular clarity and variety is the realization that a new day is dawning for them, and perhaps, for those they love or have loved.

They will soon begin the journey back to whatever places, familiar or not, they would seek. The true meaning of the experiences of the journey was not just their healing, but the strength to once again dream dreams and pursue hope, love, joy, contentment, and fulfillment.

At some point, each pilgrim descends from the top of the wall of the Grand Courtyard of The Tree. At the bottom, the ancient stone pathway leads off and down the mountain in the direction opposite of where they had come up.

There is a sign reading: "The Way of New Possibilities."

Leaving behind the walled Grand Courtyard of The Tree of Healing, each pilgrim, at her or his own pace and time, begins the journey back down the mountain. Hearts are lighter. Minds are excited about some new hope or dream or place. Some pilgrims anticipate reconciling with a loved one or friend, re-establishing a special connection long lost. Others are determined to make new friendships and longed-for relationships in the new days that lie ahead. Oft-ignored dreams and plans are resurrected along with the renewed energy to pursue them.

Some will simply find a place to continue healing and resting, especially when the journey meant uncovering and dealing with particularly deep and painful realities of their lives. They will continue on their journey later, at their own pace and in their own time.

Yet others, their lives transformed in the experience of the journey, will go back and tell others their story. For not everyone knows about The Tree of Healing of Lost Love and Missed Opportunity. They must be told!

Many others need to make the pilgrimage. Perhaps an encouraging word or the willingness to go with them to at least the beginning of the ancient stone pathway will give others the strength to do that. How could one not share this amazing experience with others, encouraging them to do the same?

Following the well-worn stone pathway down from the summit, around a bend, pilgrims begin to hear the sounds of another waterfall. As they get closer, they can clearly see the source of the soothing sounds of water cascading over a high ledge and into a magnificent pool hundreds of feet below. A truly magnificent waterfall!

The closer they get, the louder the sounds! The pilgrims remember that the springs at the foot of The Tree flowed out from the Grand Courtyard, forming two branches of the fabled River of Life. One branch goes down the mountain on the side by which pilgrims ascended, feeding The Waterfall of Understanding and nourishing the lush meadows beyond. The other branch flows in the opposite direction, forming this waterfall, before diving underground to water distant lands.

Not far from the waterfall the pathway goes behind and under the cascading torrent. There is no alternative: one must pass under and behind to get through. As pilgrims enter into the large cavern-like room behind the waterfall they cannot help but stop. The sounds of the waterfall are deafening here. The combination of sounds and water crashing into the pool below penetrate their very being. It feels like being enveloped by a million points of stimulation and energy. There is a sense of having something shaken out of the body by the strangely cleansing power of the sounds. Perhaps the sounds heard, and energy felt are, in some way or another, an unseen Higher Power re-aligning body, soul, and spirit to prepare each pilgrim for what lies ahead?

Looking toward the cascade itself, each pilgrim begins to see an image or images formed in the shimmering water. These images are spectacular. Each pilgrim can see only her or his own image or images, and no others. What each sees is unique and beyond human description. No pilgrim has words adequate.

All they can say is, "I saw a sense of my future and its new possibilities. I saw a rich, overwhelming vision. A hopeful and encouraging insight into what is coming. It will take me days, months, perhaps even years to put all that I saw into perspective. But I know what I need to do next, and I intend to do just that!"

At their own pace and in their own timing, each leaves the cavern behind the waterfall and continues down the path. Looking back at the cascading water crashing into the pool below, the angle of the sun is just right. There is a beautiful rainbow, with its glorious hues of color that perfectly frames the summit of the mountain.

Upon second look, they also see the top-most branches of The Tree of Healing of Lost Love and Missed Opportunities towering over the Grand Courtyard walls.

WHAT ASTOUNDS IS the view of The Tree through the rainbow: A part of The Tree is winter barren. Another part is in spring season. Yet another part, summer. And the rest of The Tree? Autumn. A reminder, perhaps, that the journey ahead may not be as easy as hoped, but it will be part of the larger cycle of Life. The journey ahead will have seasons that will challenge, give hope, provide fullness, and become transitions to the next chapters of each pilgrim's life.

It is also when looking through the rainbow at the mountain and The Tree that each pilgrim realizes he or she is wet. The spray from the cascading water of the River of Life has purified, anointed, in a sense baptized, each of them as they passed under the waterfall.

It is a moment of unique blessing.

All pilgrims continue their journey down the mountain at their own pace and in their own time.

Ahead, they see one last ancient, moss-covered sign along the pathway.

It reads:

"May You Keep the Peace that You Found"

About the Author

Steven Fleming has a lifetime of experience teaching, counseling, and helping people along their life journeys. Born in southern California, he grew up in Maryland. A graduate of the University of Maryland at College Park with honors in English, he received his Doctor of Ministry degree in 1976 from Union Theological Seminary in Richmond, Virginia.

A long-term cancer survivor (acute myeloid leukemia 1983-1985), he has helped people young and old explore life and its meaning serving as a spiritual leader for 21 years in Virginia, Arkansas, Pennsylvania and Maryland.

Steven has presented live seminars and workshops across the USA to thousands of persons. A gifted public speaker, writer, and seminar leader, Steven has published articles in various national publications.

He is presently pursuing his dream to provide life coaching and mentoring both via the internet, e-learning seminars and workshops, and live presentations. He would enjoy hearing from those who wish to explore their life in these possibilities.

You can find Steven on Facebook; Twitter, and LinkedIN

Go here to purchase an E-Book copy:
http://healingtreeoflostlove.com/

http://SRFLifeRetirementCoach.com

To read the blog, learn about seminars, workshops, and other resources go to:
http://healingtreeoflostlove.com

To contact Steven: mail@SRFLifeRetirementCoach.com

Made in the USA
Middletown, DE
07 July 2019